America's
**ANIMAL
COMEBACKS**

Southern Sea Otters

Fur-tastrophe Avoided

by Jeanette Leardi

Consultant: James A. Estes
Research Scientist
U.S. Geological Survey

BEARPORT
PUBLISHING

New York, New York

Credits

Cover and Title Page, © Danny Frank/SeaPics.com; 4, © Jane Vargas/SeaPics.com; 5, © Sanford/Agliolo/CORBIS; 7, © Peggy Stap/SeaPics.com; 8, Tom Suchanek/USGS; 9L, ©Sisse Brimberg/National Geographic; 9R, Courtesy of the Friends of the Sea Otter; 10, © Masa Ushioda/Stephen Frink Collection/Alamy; 10 Inset, © Daniel McCulloch/SeaPics.com; 11, © Jane Vargas/SeaPics.com; 12, © Richard Herrmann/SeaPics.com; 13, © Mark J. Rauzon/SeaPics.com; 14, USGS; 15, USGS; 16, © Doc White/SeaPics.com; 17, © Frans Lanting/Minden Pictures; 18, Calif. Dept. of Fish & Game; 19, © Jeff Foott/Discovery Channel Images/Getty Images; 20L, Tom Suchanek/USGS; 20R, ©Monterey Bay Aquarium; 21, © Steven Kazlowski/SeaPics.com; 22, © David Young-Wolff/Photo Edit; 23, © 2003 Klaus Jost/Image Quest 3-D; 24, ©Alissa Crandall/AlaskaStock.com; 25, ©David Frazier/The Image Works; 26, ©Monterey Bay Aquarium; 27, © Jane Vargas/SeaPics.com; 28, © Jane Vargas/SeaPics.com; 29T, © Phillip Colla/SeaPics.com; 29B, © Frans Lanting/Minden Pictures.

Publisher: Kenn Goin
Editorial Director: Adam Siegel
Creative Director: Spencer Brinker
Photo Researcher: Marty Levick
Cover Design: Dawn Beard Creative

Library of Congress Cataloging-in-Publication Data

Leardi, Jeanette.
 Southern sea otters : fur-tastrophe avoided / by Jeanette Leardi.
     p. cm. — (America's animal comebacks)
 Includes bibliographical references and index.
 ISBN-13: 978-1-59716-534-1 (library binding)
 ISBN-10: 1-59716-534-4 (library binding)
 1. Sea otter—Conservation—California—Juvenile literature. 2. Rare mammals—California—Juvenile literature. I. Title.

 QL737.C25.L43 2008
 599.769'5—dc22

                              2007012593

For more information, write to Bearport Publishing Company, Inc., 101 Fifth Avenue, Suite 6R, New York, New York 10003. Printed in the United States of America.

10 9 8 7 6 5 4 3 2 1

Contents

A Surprising Discovery

On March 19, 1938, Howard Sharpe was looking out at the California **coast**. From his porch, he gazed at the Pacific Ocean through his telescope. Suddenly, he saw a startling sight. About 300 small furry animals were floating on their backs in the **kelp beds**.

Southern sea otters float together in groups called rafts.

The animals looked like southern sea otters. Were Sharpe's eyes fooling him? Scientists had thought that these creatures were nearly **extinct**.

Sharpe reported his discovery to the government. A few days later, animal experts gathered at the shore and saw the **rare** creatures. One expert said he would have been almost as surprised to see live dinosaurs!

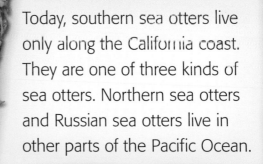

Today, southern sea otters live only along the California coast. They are one of three kinds of sea otters. Northern sea otters and Russian sea otters live in other parts of the Pacific Ocean.

5

Greedy for Fur

Sea otters were not always so rare. Between 200,000 and one million of them once made their homes along the rocky shore of the Pacific Ocean. Up to 16,000 southern sea otters lived along the western coast of the United States and parts of northern Mexico.

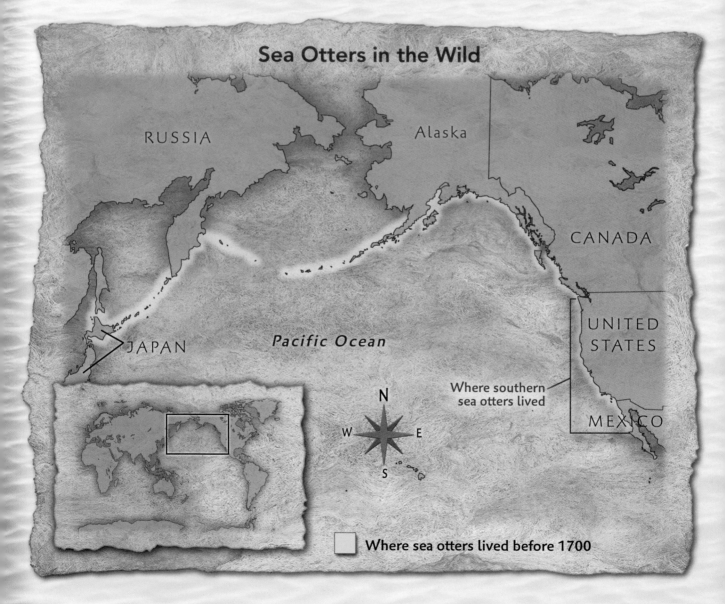

Sea Otters in the Wild

RUSSIA

Alaska

CANADA

JAPAN

Pacific Ocean

UNITED STATES

Where southern sea otters lived

MEXICO

N

W   E

S

Where sea otters lived before 1700

Then, in the 1700s, European and Russian sailors discovered the otters. They hunted the animal for its thick, warm fur.

For nearly 200 years, thousands of sea otters were killed each year. In 1911, so few were left that many countries finally agreed to stop hunting them. Yet many people believed it was too late. By 1938, some scientists thought the southern sea otter had disappeared completely. That was when Howard Sharpe made his surprising discovery.

Sea otters have the thickest fur of any animal. It keeps the small creatures warm in cold water.

One More Chance

Howard Sharpe's discovery showed that sea otters were not yet extinct. However, their numbers were very small—only around 300. Could they survive?

Scientists and **environmentalists** began a long effort to save the **species**. In 1941, California took the first step. The state set aside an area along the Pacific coast where it hoped otters could live free from harm. Creating this **refuge**, however, was not enough.

Southern Sea Otters in the Wild

N
W E
S

California

Santa Cruz

Monterey

Sea Otter
Refuge

Big Sur

Pacific
Ocean

Santa
Barbara

San Nicolas Island

UNITED
STATES

☐ Where southern sea otters
live today

This map shows where southern sea otters live today. The Sea Otter Game Refuge stretches for 100 miles (161 km) along California's coast.

By 1968, there were just 650 southern sea otters. Environmentalists Jim Mattison and Margaret Owings wanted to help the otter **population** grow faster. So that same year, they started a group called Friends of the Sea Otter.

Margaret Owings started Friends of the Sea Otter to help the playful creatures survive.

FRIENDS OF THE SEA OTTER

MONTEREY, CALIFORNIA
www.seaotters.org

Today, Friends of the Sea Otter, Defenders of Wildlife, and other groups work to pass laws that protect the sea otter and the places where it lives.

Helping Sea Otters

Friends of the Sea Otter and other environmental groups asked the U.S. government to help protect sea otters. In 1972, Congress passed the **Marine Mammal Protection Act**. The law made it **illegal** to hunt, capture, or kill sea otters. The government's goal was to find ways to increase the animal's numbers. Unfortunately, the furry creatures could not wait long for people to take action.

The Marine Mammal Protection Act protects sea otters and other mammals that live in the water. These animals include whales, seals, sea lions, and dolphins.

From the 1940s until the mid-1970s, the southern sea otter population had slowly increased. Yet in the 1970s, their numbers began to fall quickly. No one knew why. It wasn't until the early 1980s that one of the biggest problems facing sea otters was discovered—fishing nets.

In 1977, the southern sea otter population was about 1,600. That year, the government declared that the small animals could be in danger of dying out.

Caught in the Nets

In the 1970s, California had a booming fishing **industry**. Fishers used large nets to catch millions of pounds of fish and other sea creatures every year.

Unfortunately, the fishing boats worked very close to the California shore where otters lived. Their huge nets trapped anything that swam into them—including otters.

Like sea otters, sea lions were also accidentally caught in fishing nets.

Many of the small mammals could not escape from the nets and drowned. Between 1973 and 1983, fishing nets killed about 1,000 southern sea otters.

In the 1980s, the state government finally **banned** the use of big fishing nets near the shore. Hundreds of otters' lives were saved.

A sea otter caught in a fishing net

Sea otters cannot breathe underwater like fish. When otters get trapped in fishing nets, many of them die because they are not able to reach the surface to get air.

A New Home

Once sea otters were protected from fishing nets, more of them survived. Yet they were still in danger.

Most of the animals lived in waters close to oil **tankers**. What if a spill happened? Almost all the otters could be wiped out. So scientists came up with a plan. They would try moving some otters to a new location. If animals in one place were harmed, others would still be safe.

The otter in this crate was captured and flown to the coast of San Nicolas Island.

Between 1987 and 1990, scientists moved 139 otters to the coast of San Nicolas Island. It was hoped they would live and **breed** there.

Some otters did not survive the move. Many others tried to return to their old home. Yet today, about 50 otters live around the island.

A sea otter on San Nicolas Island

San Nicolas Island is located about 70 miles (113 km) west of Los Angeles, California. The number of sea otters there is now growing.

A Special Species

Scientists did not give up trying to save sea otters. They were learning how important the animals are to the ocean's **ecosystem**.

Sea otters float, eat, and sleep in kelp beds. Kelp is also food and shelter for snails, fish, and spiny animals called sea urchins. Without enough otters, some of these animals could be in danger. Why?

Sea otters wrap themselves in kelp to keep from drifting away as they eat or sleep.

Sea urchins eat kelp. The otters then eat the sea urchins. If there are not enough otters, too many sea urchins will survive. The urchins will eat too much kelp. Not enough of the plants will be left for other sea animals to eat or use as a shelter. Many of them will starve and die.

Scientists call sea otters a "keystone species" because they are key to balancing their ecosystem.

Sea urchins are a favorite food of sea otters.

Keeping Track

Scientists want to keep track of how the furry animals are doing. So every spring and fall, research teams visit the California shore. For weeks, they count all the otters they find. Some **researchers** fly in planes to find them.

Researchers capture otters to learn more about them.

The first count in 1982 turned up around 1,300 otters. After fishing nets stopped catching the furry animals, their numbers grew. By 1995, there were more than 2,300. Researchers hoped that otters would soon no longer be in danger of dying out.

Then the population started to drop. By 1999, it was down to 2,090. Why was this happening?

The best time for researchers to count otters is between 9:00 A.M. and 2:00 P.M. During that time, most sea otters are resting on top of the water instead of diving below for food.

Pups at Risk

To solve the mystery of the otters' shrinking numbers, scientists closely studied the animals. Researchers captured otters and examined them. They put a tiny radio **transmitter** inside each animal before they released it. Then they could track the otters' movements.

A radio transmitter

Researchers are going to place a radio transmitter inside this otter's body.

Scientists soon discovered a big problem. Not enough baby otters were surviving. Since the 1990s, up to half of all **pups** were dying. In addition, many young females died before they could have babies. As a result, fewer pups were being born. "When we start losing breeding females, that's not . . . healthy," said Mike Murray, who works at the Monterey Bay Aquarium.

Female sea otters usually only have one pup at a time. When they are born, pups weigh three to five pounds (1–2 kg).

Otter pups depend on their mothers for food and protection.

Deadly Pollution

Why were so many pups and young otters dying? Scientists haven't figured out all the reasons. Part of the answer, however, is water **pollution**.

Each year, children and adults in California take part in the state's Coastal Cleanup Day. They help keep beaches and other shore areas from becoming polluted.

In 2006, California passed a new law to reduce the amount of pet waste dumped into the ocean. This law will help keep the sea otter's home cleaner.

Poisonous **pesticides** from farms wash into areas where otters swim. Waste from humans and pets also wash into the sea, carrying with it deadly diseases. These poisons and diseases can make otters very sick and die.

The great white shark is another danger to sea otters. Many of the furry creatures die from shark attacks.

A Big Victory

One of the most dangerous kinds of water pollution threatening otters is oil. In 1992, a broken **pipeline** near Avila Beach spilled 600 barrels of oil onto the California shore. The spill put nearby otters in terrible danger.

In 1989, the ship *Exxon Valdez* spilled 11 million gallons (42 million liters) of oil off the coast of Alaska. The disaster killed more than 3,500 northern sea otters.

Rescuers clean oil from the coat of an otter caught in the *Exxon Valdez* oil spill in Alaska.

When oil coats otters' fur, they cannot stay warm. The animals may die from the cold water. They can also become sick from licking the oil as they try to clean themselves.

In 2005, environmentalists won a big victory. They blocked companies from drilling for oil in 36 places off the California coast. This will help protect southern sea otters from more oil spills.

This oil rig is drilling for oil in the ocean near Long Beach, California. Today, laws ban oil drilling close to the California shore where otters live.

The Future

Otters are not yet out of danger. In spring 2006, researchers counted 2,692 animals. Southern sea otters will remain threatened until their population reaches at least 3,000 animals.

These people are learning more about sea otters by watching them in action at the Monterey Bay Aquarium.

In California, it is against the law to harm sea otters. Anyone who kills a sea otter must pay the government a fine of $25,000.

There may not be enough sea otters yet. However, there are many more today than the 300 that Howard Sharpe found in 1938. Cleaner waters and protected **habitats** have given otters safer places to live, too.

Scientists and environmentalists continue working to keep the furry creatures safe. With people's help, the playful animals can have a bright future along the California coast.

Southern Sea Otter Facts

In 1973, Congress passed the **Endangered** Species Act. This law protects animals and plants that are in danger of dying out in the United States. Harmful activities, such as hunting, capturing, or collecting endangered species, are illegal under this act.

In 1977, the southern sea otter was listed as threatened under the Endangered Species Act. Here are some other facts about the southern sea otter.

Population: **Population in 1700:** up to 16,000
Population in spring 2006: 2,692

Weight
females: 40–55 pounds (18–25 kg)
males: 60–75 pounds (27–34 kg)

Length
females: 4 feet (1.2 m)
males: 4–4.5 feet (1.2–1.4 m)

Fur Color
dark brown body, head may be white or blond

Food
different kinds of sea animals, including abalone, crabs, clams, mussels, octopuses, and sea urchins

Life Span
females: 15–20 years
males: 10–15 years

Habitat
California coast

Other Marine Mammals in Danger

The southern sea otter is one kind of marine mammal making a comeback by increasing its numbers. Other marine mammals are also trying to make a comeback.

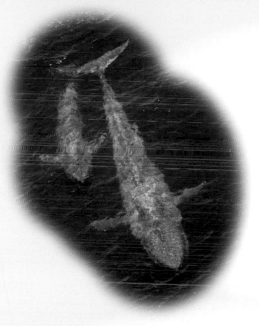

Blue Whale

- There are fewer than 5,000 blue whales in the world.

- Blue whales are the largest animals on Earth. They live in every ocean.

- They are in danger from illegal hunting, fishing nets, and pollution.

- Since 1965, many countries have agreed to protect the whales.

Hawaiian Monk Seal

- There are between 1,200 and 1,400 Hawaiian monk seals in the world.

- They live around the Hawaiian Islands.

- Hawaiian monk seals are in danger from fishing nets, disease, predators, and pollution.

- Scientists are studying the seals, cleaning up their habitat, and keeping them safe from threats like sharks.

Glossary

banned (BAND) did not allow

breed (BREED) to produce young

coast (KOHST) land that runs along an ocean

ecosystem (EE-koh-*siss*-tuhm) a community of animals and plants that depend on one another to live

endangered (en-DAYN-jurd) in danger of dying out

environmentalists (en-*vye*-ruhn-MEN-tuhl-ists) people who work to protect plants and animals

extinct (ek-STINGKT) when a kind of plant or animal has died out; no more of its kind is living anywhere in the world

habitats (HAB-uh-*tats*) places in nature where animals normally live

illegal (i-LEE-guhl) against the law

industry (IN-duh-*stree*) the businesses and companies that make, sell, or trade a particular thing to make money

kelp beds (KELP BEDZ) floating groups of a sea plant called kelp

marine mammal (muh-REEN MAM-uhl) a warm-blooded animal that lives in the water, has hair or fur on its skin, and drinks its mother's milk as a baby

pesticides (PESS-tuh-*sidez*) poisonous chemicals used to kill insects and other pests

pipeline (PIPE-*line*) a system of pipes that moves oil over long distances

pollution (puh-LOO-shuhn) gases, liquids, or objects that harm the living things in an environment

population (*pop*-yuh-LAY-shuhn) the total number of a kind of animal living in a place

pups (PUHPS) baby sea otters; short for "puppies"

rare (RAIR) not often found or seen

refuge (REF-yooj) a place that provides shelter or protection for animals

researchers (REE-sur-churz) people who study things or collect information

species (SPEE-sheez) groups that animals are divided into, according to similar characteristics; members of the same species can have offspring together

tankers (TANG-kurz) ships that carry liquids, such as oil

transmitter (tranz-MIT-ur) a device that sends out radio waves to help scientists track an animal

Bibliography

Ellis, Richard. *The Empty Ocean: Plundering the World's Marine Life.* Washington, D.C.: Island Press (2003).

Hildyard, Anne, ed. "Southern Sea Otter," in *Endangered Wildlife and Plants of the World,* vol. 7. New York: Marshall Cavendish (2001).

Jessup, David, D.V.M. "Southern Sea Otter: Sentinel of the Sea," *Outdoor California* (September/October 2003), 4–13.

www.defenders.org/wildlife/new/seaotters.html

www.dfg.ca.gov

Read More

Brust, Beth Wagner. *Sea Otters.* Poway, CA: Wildlife Education, Ltd. (2001).

Hirschmann, Kris. *Sea Otters.* Detroit, MI: KidHaven Press (2005).

Kalman, Bobbie. *Sea Otters.* New York: Crabtree Publishing (1996).

León, Vicki. *A Raft of Sea Otters: The Playful Life of a Furry Survivor.* Montrose, CA: London Town Press (2005).

Learn More Online

To learn more about southern sea otters, visit
www.bearportpublishing.com/AnimalComebacks

Index

About the Author

Jeanette Leardi has written many educational books for children, and poems, articles, and essays for adults. She is the author of *The Great Pyramid: Egypt's Tomb for All Time*.